Above the Sky Beneath the Earth

Above the Sky Beneath the Earth

Aleš Šteger

Translated from the Slovenian by Brian Henry

WHITE PINE PRESS / BUFFALO, NEW YORK

White Pine Press
P.O. Box 236
Buffalo, NY 14201
www.whitepine.org

Publication of this book was supported in part by grants from the Trubar Foundation and the Slovenian Book Agency (JAK).

JAK SLOVENIAN BOOK AGENCY

The author and translator wish to acknowledge the publishers who first brought the following poems into print:

The Brooklyn Rail: "Like a virgin forest," "The master's spiders," "A person is a shadow," "A person isn't a spot," "The sun is stuck."
Field: "He writes."
Jubilat: "Transit."
The Laurel Review: "The Lord said."
New American Writing: "Father is the outcome," "I have a white shirt," "My body is a Central Committee."
NPR's Morning Edition: "If a great idea is translated."
Poetry International: "As in sex," "Reason has a wish."

Printed and bound in the United States of America.

Cover image: *Migrant Universe: Landscape and Departure* by Tanja Softić. Copyright ©2019 by Tanja Softić.

ISBN 978-1-945680-32-8

Library of Congress number 2018968433

Contents

Beneath the earth

Field of audibility

Sky and Earth and I were born at the same time and all life and I are one. What is the need for words if all life is one? I just said that all life is one, so I already spoke, didn't I? One and the word is two, two and one is three. Continuing this thought surpasses the abilities of the most skilled mathematician …

—Zhuangzi

Beneath the Earth

Here comes the boy who plays
On a halogen light.
Because of the noise
Nothing can be seen.
In fetid cellars he leaves behind
Plasters and fish oil.
This is not a metaphysical era.
This is not an era for the voice.
This is the era of halogenic noise.
Unplug the herring from your ears.
Can you smell my fear?
The forecast sets
In a broken puddle.
Our era began
Like a toothache.
It will end with the hallucinations
Of microbes in the dark.

A scene in a tavern.
A witch blows out a lantern.
Pursues *danmari,*
A stylized struggle in the dark.
The stage is lit,
The actors see
But are in the dark.
Like us,
Who sit in the audience,
Like us,
When the performance ends,
In life.

Esteemed doctor of culture!
Birds fly beneath the roots.
Computers are sweating.
At the poles, holes grow,
And deaf-mute people rush
From inside them
To scrape the sclera
And shame from our eyes.
Our names are proteins.
We are happy when we burn them.
Cherished doctor,
Internationally ill expert
On the manufacture of souls.
Without a doubt we are dialogic.
Whoever doubts goes in the pit,
Whoever doesn't doubt goes the only way.
No doctrines. The time of salvation is already
Breathing down a dirty neck.
The day arrives like a poem
In a lost language.
A barefoot girl is pricked
By a forgotten word
And gnashes her teeth.

Love is
A small kitten
Drinking water
From a cracked dish.

He writes, places marks, becomes excited,
Wastes his whole life on an apparently useless activity.

No one notices his undertaking.
Children run around, unaware they erase his efforts.

Despite everything, he's convinced that the fate of the universe
Is in his hands, depends on his persistence.

What was uncovered countless times
Will be uncovered again.

His activity prolongs the word *foam,*
The word *fan,* the word *this,* the word *presence.*

It prolongs the artful veiling
That accompanies the seducer, poetry.

Weary bathers shake out the towels
They were lying on all day on the sand.

What remains is an impression that will be erased again and again.
What there is is the revolt against the end of summer.

Time is a migratory bird.
Man has
The genome of a stone.

Between truth and man
I choose waiting.

Between waiting and man
I choose plastic flowers.

I am not foolish,
Wanting to be a genius.

All I want is
The stiff penises of meteorologists.

May they forecast precisely,
Preventing the slaughter of my Isaac.

Three haiku
By the stream at Ryoanji
Temple in Kyoto

1.

Moss, moss, gravel and dust.
Beneath the earth man and cloud
Are leveled.

2.

Under the gravel, signs.
Nearby, moss overgrows
Your address on Earth.

3.

A flag writes in the air
The names of the nameless.
Moss is wisely silent.

for Ilma Rakusa

Were you there?
Yes, a voice says.

Did you also do
The same bad things?

Yes, a voice says.
You're crying.

Where are they, those
Who could forgive you?

Are you really alone in the world?
The voice is silent.

The master's spiders are weaving
A wireless network around us.

Someone on another continent
Secretly reads our thoughts.

Through the door nothing is visible.
In the dark we are smaller than gnats.

My palms reach for you,
Sink into a veiled mirror.

When I finally reach you,
I embrace the whole world.

If a great idea is translated into a body,
Then Greg Louganis is an Einstein.

If a body is translated into a great idea,
Einstein is *tralala oompah.*

Which gods do chess grandmasters dream about?

My love, it is time we all participate
In this outrageous activity.

Let bankers with pacemakers run the marathon.
Let naked sumo wrestlers decide our common fate.

Let us pierce the concrete with our heads.

Every time it's a top score
And we are in no hurry to get anywhere.

The Lord said Mountain.
Snow fell and covered the Lord.

The Lord called Spring
And it came running out of the mountain.

The Lord disappeared into the tops of pines.
Summer blazed on the surface of the lake.

The Lord watched a man
Who bathed himself in the Lord.

O   E
Murmured the Lord.

How much of the Lord has to pass by
So that one solemn man becomes purified.

A professor has proven
That human history is
The history of a continuous decrease in violence.
Cruel cavemen, wild nomads, peasant uprisings.
Nowadays we're only concerned with
Raw food, social networks, gender equality.
There is barely enough violence in the world
To fill the daily newspapers,
The professor says thoughtfully,
And with a quick motion of his right palm
He slaughters the mosquito that was sitting
On the crease of his pressed pants.

Someone
Goes to hell
And back.

Chasms, monsters, trials.

The place where he loses his shoes
Lends him a name.

My body is a Central Committee.
The blood is the Party's cell for religious and ideological questions.
You dream too materialistically,
My Komsomol comrades tease me.
In order to be better, I grab my soul
And hurl it over the threshold.
Let it disappear until the next Congress, only so there's peace.
But soon it flutters back, wanders around,
Knocks over chairs and leafs through the books of my Chinese comrades.
It would like to be one of them and die smoothly.
Thus I must deal with
Destroying the intangible plot of our future.
In the next life I will choose other ancestors,
A more courteous environment, feed on roots,
Die like a stone on the grate of a hydroelectric plant.
But as a European I hang onto my soul
Like mass killings hang on the testicles of revolution.
The soul returns from church. Says that the flame of the funeral candle is beautiful.
I hurl it into the crematory. Scorch its wings.
It returns shaken up, shouts that fire is a dreadful class enemy.
I hurl it into the last circle of hell.
From there it communicates no signs.
What good practice and eons teach:
1. The Party must adopt
An eternal moratorium on the souls of the dead returning.
2. The Party must reward
Self-immolation and other bodily pleasures.
3. The Party must become mystical
Toward death, like my name is in relation
To cells, from which it disappears
Without ever living in them.

Field of Audibility

Transit

Tokyo

A wall grows next to another
Like the nights in Shinagawa.

The passage is too narrow
For the fireflies of words.

I got stuck in silence,
So I write.

Ljubljana

For twenty years I've watched
Hornets battle
Above an empty trash can.
I live
Under its rusted bottom.

Kyoto

Even without Kyoto,
Without suitcases and longing,
I miss Basho.

Berlin

Needles grow from windowsills.
We're protected from birds.

A cold July wind
Scatters dead souls.

No possibility of rest.
And you, who loves all this.

Chengdu

The buzz of a plane
Crosses a garden
With a thatched cottage.

Tu Fu once
Found refuge here
From war.

Time is a gap-toothed old woman
Silently awaiting him
At the door.

Guadalajara

Dogs sleeping in the sand.
Like silent mariachis
Memories come and go.
I'm staying.

Nicosia

I hear ripe oranges
Falling into mud.
People, cordoned off by the sea,
Braid barbed wire.
The one and only God
Is also singing
Infinite truths for us
In infinite languages.
Five times a day.

Buenos Aires

21st floor.
The city is an old woman
In black velvet.

Letters on a sheet of paper,
Ants covering
Anonymous prey.

Only this is certain:
No one is praying anymore.
No one is breathing anymore.

A siren cuts through the horizon
Like a blind tailor
With rusty scissors.

Eyes closed, I offer thanks.
We are saved
For another day.

Beijing

In Beijing
All poetry is
Misty,
Above and below.
The sun
Mid-day,
The dark
Inside me
Are one.

Transit code

Suvarnabhumi,
Shangri-la,
You and your monkey.

Doha, Beijing,
Shanghai
Again into the foreign world nearby.

There is one seat, one flight coupon,
Only one suitcase, one bonbon.

Houston, Stansted, Mérida,
Lima, Tivat and Sana'a.

In one head always two,
You and your monkey.

Qu'est-ce que la poésie?

A weed.

Then
The inevitable question,
Which plows up
What is before language.

Behind the plow, processions
Of enraptured philosophers.

But from where?
But why?

I repeat: a weed.

I am astonished by
The certainty of the claim.

Whose?

I repeat:
No questions!

A person isn't a spot.
A person is a tail.
In absolute reality
All scenarios
Are possible.
Our spectrum
Is the strait.
We are all,
But at the same time
All possibilities
Aren't for us.
Oh, my lovely blinders!
Oh, my gorgeous tail!
Oh, the past,
Which sits on me like
A fly on a nose.
Fate gives us
Unbearable freedom.
That's why I'd rather
Pull and pull
The whole world like a puzzle
That I created.
No, a person isn't a spot.
Truth isn't a horse.
I affirm this, unshod
And under no duress.

At the circus I got
A magic square.
Nine symbols.
Their sum always death.

Mother sent me
To your unknown
Residence
For a reading.

Before I even learned
Where to search,
I became the shape
Of your absence.

The umbilical cord still hangs
Between the abandoned telegraph poles.
The whole world is a uterus.
The living and the dead send
Wireless messages.

My mother
Who art in bodies,
Devastation is your name.
Come to me at least
In your exile,
Your brutality occurs
In poverty and plenty.
Toss today at least
A worthless crumb
And forgive me
My moments of weakness,
When I try to steal more from life
Than you intend.
Don't lead me once more into emptiness,
May my bones be crushed
When you caress me,
Mother.

A poet is born
When she hears a voice.

The voice is immortal.
It is here. Permanently
On loan.

For a moment the chirping of a blackbird
Drowns out the roar of the crowd.

Love is an unstitched thread.
The textile industry is sacred.

Where did you hear this?
In my ear.

A mistake is
A part of perfection.
A lie, a part of the truth.

But why does a caterpillar try
To become a butterfly?

As in sex,
The body of the other
In poetry
Is mystically unattainable.

There are no laws,
Only farewells.

One must abandon
All words,
As water in a delta abandons
The riverbed
That led it safely
Over land.

Two tongues made out of rain
Will spell with water,
In water, out of the water
You are, you are.

Thank you.

Milk turns to ash.
History to oblivion.
A deer eats a weed
In the garden of my
Dead mother.

Father is the outcome of my words.
He grows in test tubes and clouds.
The door of guilt and a private curse.
I tell him: up yours.
He goes, peers out through a mouth.
Life is an ellipse and an oxymoron.
It has no more than five words.
First: love is the indifference of meteorology.
There's nothing wrong with rain.
Second: the world is without culprits.
My stammering spells the periodic table.
Third: to be free on the farm of the gods.
Happiness is when I shovel.
Fourth: I'm always repeating my father again.
He grows like cavities and architecture.
Fifth: there is no justice, only revolution.
The oxymoron is life in an ellipse.
It has no more than five words.
The sixth sticks deep in the throat.
And the seventh is, reportedly, indigestible and silent.
The elliptical oxymoron of life.

An evolutionary truth.
One fractioned
By Darwin.
Man is evolving
Into monkey.
There are no bananas
Waiting for me there.

From palms
Bloody from
St. John's wort
And drunken grapes
I received the news
That everything is related
And is simultaneously
Good and evil.

Woe is me.
What does clay turn into,
What does breath,
When will sweet snow
Cover me?

Every one of us
Is from somewhere,
Everyone is endlessly
Arriving
From somewhere.

We'll never stop
Arriving, singing, being everyone.

Stars, rivers, mountains
Are unreliable orientation.

Only what you carry,
What you cannot stop
Carrying inside yourself
When you're arriving and arriving
Endlessly,
It is only this,
Only this—
The only place.

Everything from somewhere,
Everyone, someplace.

You'll be praised,
The undefinable and free
Course of our path.

The sun is stuck
In the crown of a century-old oak.

If only I too could
Recline always awake

In its clear shadow,
The sky in my eyes.

Above the Sky

I have a white shirt.
In the middle of the night
A dark body glows in it.

White is the border.
I live here.
I am spoken there.

I have a white,
Snowy,
Angelic shirt.

I raise the collar.
Unfasten a button.
Roll up a sleeve.

Language gets dirty.
The angel gets dirty.
The soul gets dirty.

But I still live
In my snowy clean,
In my perfectly white shirt.

Look how the mountains arise!
Mountains don't arise, the mountains are.

Look, rain is being made!
But rain isn't made, rain is.

Look, a day is being born.
But a day isn't born, a day is.

I ran through this meadow like a child.
Now my aged son walks through it.

But it wasn't me running.
I am.

Like a virgin forest
We too have become coal.

You, who goes into yourself,
Remember the echoes.

Whoever digs into time
Injures eternity.

Reason has a wish
But cannot control
My destiny.

The soul can control
Destiny,
But it has no will.

I tuck reason
Into a black briefcase
And my soul behind an ear.

As I walk alone
The black briefcase rattles.
Someone is whispering to me.

A person is a shadow
Thrown by a letter.
The letter goes everywhere.
The shadow doesn't leave
The cave.

I did not throw myself into the crater of Mount Etna
Or into the voracious mouth of Pantagruel.

I planted lindens in the desert sand. Dug graves in silence.
Nothing grew. No one echoed.

The sight of silent oracles and fog dealers
Fed me bitter honey when I was weak.

I did not regret. I am a decaying descent
In the direction of an opaque reflection. Whose, I don't know.

When we meet, the sound of the sea will be my pillow,
The shadow of a seagull on my eyelid.

According to esoteric theories
The human aura is infinite,
Though with distance increasingly diluted.

I just brushed against someone
On the other side of the universe.
And on the contrary, I'm touching everything.

How many encounters, how much inevitability!
It's good that my mind is limited
And my name is untranslatable.

Sometimes it grows dark on earth.
Your home deep in dusk.
Behind a window curtain, like a mirage,
A tiny light in the dark.

Whoever thinks hope misses it.
It flickers so that you sense your shadow,
A blind Tiresias who soaks his fingers
In the blackness of letters. Feels the cracks. Follows.

When I speak, I give birth to chaos.
It climbs from my mouth.
Words only conceal it temporarily.
The gust of time blows them away.
Chaos stands up and grows.
May my eye not close
When my Polyphemus swallows me.

To do nothing,
I don't dare.
It's awful,
What all this
Little nothing
Does with a man.
It's better to escape
Into words,
Where the big little man
And the minuscule
Immense nothing
Are tamed.
Even if a word sometimes
Backs you into a dead corner,
There is always a door.
Who can
Write what is
Behind this door?

There's a place in you
Where you secretly live,
Forbidden shards,
A place where
No one may go.

Nothing sweeter
Than being
A passing doe
That's licking this place
With a bleeding tongue.

Shall I fall into the gray sky,
Into the pale stroke in the gray,

Into the trace that, behind a feeling, reveals
That it does not exist, and thus will return.

Shall I fall, vanish into the in-between
Like a mouse into the floor of night, sleepless.

And never awaken except in letters.
Shall I fall and fall and leave

Because I love returning, because I am
Above the sky, beneath the earth, forever.

A poem nests
In my head.
Where is its home?
Everywhere.
When does it exist?
Always.
If all poems are
Always everywhere,
How do I know
That the poem
In my head
Is really mine?
Cheeepcheepcheepcheeeep
It mockingly cheeps
In an unreachable
Tree.

Son,
When you wake up,
Horses continue to run
Through your dreams.

Five assertions,
This is all
The years have washed up.

First: I loved you
Even before I existed.

Second: my life
Is a drop of black ink in the boundless night.

Third: There is no end,
Only snow-covered mountain peaks.

Fourth: The sea doesn't
Care about us.

Last: There is no end,
Only glaciers are dying.

Slovenian writer Aleš Šteger has published seven books of poetry, three novels, and two books of essays. A Chevalier des Artes et Lettres in France and a member of the Berlin Academy of Arts, he received the 1998 Veronika Prize for the best Slovenian poetry book, the 1999 Petrarch Prize for young European authors, the 2007 Rožanc Award for the best Slovenian book of essays, and the 2016 International Bienek Prize. His work has been translated into over fifteen languages, including Chinese, German, Czech, Croatian, Hungarian, and Spanish. He has published four books in English: *The Book of Things, Berlin, Essential Baggage,* and the novel *Absolution.* He also has worked in the field of visual arts (most recently with a large scale installation at the International Kochi-Muziris Biennale in India), completed several collaborations with musicians (Godalika, Uroš Rojko, Peter N. Gruber), and collaborated with Peter Zach on the film *Beyond Boundaries.*

Author photograph by Bernard Aichner.

About the translator

Brian Henry is the author of ten books of poetry. He has translated books by Tomaž Šalamun, Aleš Šteger, and Aleš Debeljak. His poetry and translations have received numerous honors, including an NEA fellowship, a Howard Foundation grant, the Alice Fay di Castagnola Award, the Carole Weinstein Poetry Prize, the Cecil B. Hemley Memorial Award, the Best Translated Book Award, and the George Bogin Memorial Award.